Ex Libris

Worldly Virtues

Johannes A. Gaertner

Viking

VIKING
Published by the Penguin Group
Penguin Books USA Inc., 375 Hudson Street,
New York, New York 10014, U.S.A.
Penguin Books Ltd, 27 Wrights Lane,
London W8 5TZ, England
Penguin Books Australia Ltd, Ringwood,
Victoria, Australia
Penguin Books Canada Ltd, 10 Alcorn Avenue,
Toronto, Ontario, Canada M4V 3B2
Penguin Books (N.Z.) Ltd, 182–190 Wairau Road,
Auckland 10, New Zealand

Penguin Books Ltd, Registered Offices:
Harmondsworth, Middlesex, England

Published in 1994 by Viking Penguin,
a division of Penguin Books USA Inc.

1 3 5 7 9 10 8 6 4 2

This work was previously published in a limited edition.

ISBN 0-670-85392-5
CIP data available

Printed in the United States of America
Set in Nicholas Cochin
Designed by Brian Mulligan

Introduction

This book was born in 1990 as a Christmas present for my father. Having found the manuscript of this book among his papers, I thought my publishing it would be a fitting tribute as well as an ideal gift for his friends and admirers, many of them former students from his forty years of teaching.

My father is one of a dying breed: the European émigré humanist in whom vocation and avocation, learning for a living and living for learning run in perfect, parallel harmony. Having begun his training as a theologian and linguist, my father segued into art history and aesthetics as time and tenure permitted. Along the way he taught everything from music appreciation to middle high

German, from Latin to ethics. The diverse strands of his erudition and inclination have produced the observations which follow. As his daughter, I'd grown up surrounded with these ideas; they were as natural as the food on our table. Little did I dream, however, what a responsive chord they would strike in others. . . .

The original volume, entitled *Worldly Wisdom: A Catalog of Virtues* and published privately in an edition of one thousand by friends in Cologne, was warmly received by friends and acquaintances. Clearly, a wider audience beckoned. I took the book to Stuart Bernstein of Endicott Booksellers in Manhattan and the rest is history: the book sold as quickly as Stuart could stock it. Now Viking Penguin has made it available for all.

– Susanna B. Gaertner

Preface to the First Edition

This compendium of singular qualities, the result of seven decades of a reflective, yet engaged life in diverse countries and cultures, adds up to a world view which many will find comforting and familiar, others unsettling and strange. With its deceptively simple prose, *Worldly Virtues* takes on the fuzziness of current public and private behavior, positing a canon of human characteristics which are instantly recognizable. No startling revelations blaze forth from these pages, rather, a calm and careful sequence of those traits by which we might articulate our being. In an age of moral relativism, even positive traits can be lost through lack of attention, lack of definition. *Worldly Virtues* provides those definitions, sharpening images, rendering a clear profile. Very simply, *Worldly Virtues* articulates moral posture.

By giving voice to the forms and shapes of human behavior, the author makes possible a ready acceptance—or rejection—of the phases and phrases by which we identify ourselves. Even if you know what you are about to read, having it clearly and firmly stated brings these elemental factors into brighter focus. We can all benefit from such an illumination.

May each reader find here a chuckle, a charge, a convivial heartbeat.

— *Susanna B. Gaertner*

Worldly

Virtues

Deliberateness—

Difficult to achieve for those who have a quick and teeming mind. It means keeping one's mind unto the matter at hand and not letting it stray away; to do whatever one does slowly, carefully, consciously. This is a winter exercise, good for the days of snow and slush, for times of introspection and recollection. Thought imbuing action, brief meditation preceding every deed, gathering oneself: first thinking, then willing, then doing. Too much of it becomes affectation, but only if the aim and purpose of the deliberate word or deed is the impression it makes upon others, not its intrinsic usefulness, beauty, or goodness.

Perseverance—

Too little of it makes men flighty, weak, unsuccessful, and insubstantial; too much of it makes them obstinate, fanatical, destructive, and even suicidal. My father used to say that it takes less to die a quick and glorious death on the battlefield than to call reveille every morning at 5:30 and not miss a single time for thirty years. To persevere means to be severe to oneself until one has accomplished what one has set out to do. It is a virtue that finds small regard in an age of flexibility, accommodation, expediency, and that cheap capitulation before any difficulty which we call "being realistic."

Sensitivity—

A term made fashionable these days by those who blame others for not being sensitive enough to perceive the evils and injustices wrought upon the helpless poor, the very young and the very old, and some minorities. The eighteenth century spoke of sensibility and thought it a hallmark of higher nature and refinement. The total absence of moral sensitivity is indeed frightening and occurs in psychotic criminals who are unable to imagine or to experience sympathetically the suffering they inflict upon their victims. Yet sensitivity alone is not enough; we also need courage, energy, and determination. Shedding tears is only a start.

Reverence

We consider its opposite, irreverence, as virtue today. There are times when the bold breaking of tablets and smashing of idols is appropriate and necessary, but our time is not one of those. Too much has been destroyed and the safety which those tablets and idols once provided is ours no longer. Goethe wanted all education to be founded upon reverence. It matters little who or what the object of our reverence is: God, Buddha, Christ, Nature, St. Francis, or the rabbi next door, provided the soul can feel awe, fear, love, and humility before something better, greater, more significant than itself. True community exists where people share their reverence.

Virtue—

An obsolete term, slightly pompous and preachy. According to Lichtenberg, an eighteenth-century aphorist, the virtue of women is three inches long. And, indeed, there were times when a woman could be stupid, vain, and lazy provided she was "pure" before marriage and "virtuous" thereafter. Virtue for both sexes, however, meant at all times fulfilling an *a priori* existing set of rules for perfect behavior, if not surpassing it. A standard of probity, decency, and moral obligation tacitly was acknowledged by all. We have lost—not entirely, but to a large extent—that standard, that common inner knowledge and in that sense cannot be virtuous in the way our forebears were.

Frugality—

Voluntary poverty. "I've been rich and I've been poor and, believe me, rich is better," is a quip attributed to an American actress, which has the charm of stating what everyone thinks and nobody says. Nevertheless: she may have been wrong. Poverty imposed is terrible, poverty chosen is marvelous. It unclutters our lives, it is healthier and safer than wealth, it frees us from many anxieties, it puts a stop to the incredible squandering of all our resources. The monks who chose chastity, obedience, and poverty meant to live happier lives. And did so in most cases. Frugality is not a penance, but an enhancement of life, a getting rid of superfluities, a turning to fundamentals, a source of joy.

Kindliness

The doorbell rang. The man who was finishing his breakfast hurried to open the door. Two women stood there, one of whom said that she belonged to a certain sect and that she wanted to talk to him. The man, who was leaving for his office and who knew the views of this sect anyhow, replied that he and his wife were busy at the moment and added, "But thank you for coming." An act of love would have been to try to convert the woman to his own view, an act of kindness would have been to buy one of her pamphlets, an act of kindliness was what he did. Kindliness is the façade of kindness, but that façade is also important.

Tact

Implies the awareness of another person's feelings, the anticipation of his reactions, and the adroit removal or avoidance of psychological difficulties and social frictions. Tact is less a function of feeling than one of intelligence. If women are said to be more tactful than men, it is because they are more intelligent, particularly with regard to human relations. (Baby girls smile earlier than baby boys.) Tact requires what Rudolf Steiner called "moral phantasy." One must be able not only to see but to feel the world as another might, thus not merely refraining from saying the wrong thing but sometimes actually not saying or doing the right thing. Tact is the courtesy of the heart.

Gratitude

Is tripartite: social, moral, and spiritual. To say thank you for a favor received or to show appreciation in some other way constitutes the social aspect of gratitude. To return a favor, to compensate one good deed with another characterizes the moral side of gratitude. To adopt gratitude as the basic tenor of one's life—gratitude for being alive, for being free, healthy, and intelligent, gratitude for the senses and their pleasures, the mind and its adventures, the soul and its delights—is to have discovered the highest and ultimate function of gratitude. To speak gratitude is courteous and pleasant, to enact gratitude is generous and noble, but to live gratitude is to touch Heaven.

Obedience—

A non-virtue today, to our great loss. Americans always confound obedience with lack of pride, with obsequiousness, servility, and other deficiencies. We are willing—in theory—to follow rules, but not men. Yet that is self-deception. Rules are not only made, they are enforced by and embodied in persons: judges, teachers, parents, policemen, bureaucrats, bosses, roommates, and fraternity brothers. These are the people we follow, not any abstract norms. If the one whom we follow is inspiring, obedience is sheer joy. We need better leaders, not better laws. Without knowing it, most of us crave obedience. If nothing else, obedience frees us from responsibility. As sacrifice, obedience ennobles. It seldom destroys and often enhances personality.

Humor—

Meaning good humor. Many claim it, few have it. Also: what is funny to men is not always funny to women and vice versa. Humor is the ability to perceive something amusing in most situations, to endure with a smile, not to take oneself too seriously. I once sat in a crowded airplane returning from Europe. While we were over the Atlantic, one of the engines suddenly stopped. The captain announced that, due to mechanical failure, we would now return to Ireland. There was an awful silence in the cabin, then one young voice said calmly and distinctly, "The rubber band broke." Everyone laughed and the tension dissolved. However hackneyed, it is still true: Laugh and the world laughs with you; weep and you weep alone.

Cheerfulness—

The outward expression of joy and good will. Joy is a precious gift, but it is for ourselves alone; we share it with others by cheerfulness. Good cheer exerts a magnetic attraction. Cheerfulness is infectious, it radiates and warms. The ugliest face becomes attractive through cheerfulness. It is not by clowning, by cracking jokes or performing parlor tricks that we make people love or like us but by an even temper, a ready smile, a benevolent disposition, and a cheerful manner. As the Christmas carol says, "God rest ye merry gentlemen, let nothing you dismay," or the Bible: "Be of good cheer," which is not an admonition but a command.

Gaiety

Cheerfulness is smiling, gaiety is jubilant. One is like wine perhaps, the other like champagne. Gaiety is bubbling, "bursting out all over," exuberant, though not as steady and enduring as cheerfulness. It is often found in healthy children and depends upon many things, health foremost, happiness, lack of worries—ultimately, however, it is simply a blessing bestowed upon us. Cheerfulness is glowing, gaiety is a fire brightly burning. Alas, like fire, like love, like life itself, gaiety consumes its own substance. By definition, it cannot last forever and should not be provoked, prolonged, or stimulated by artifice or excess.

Joy

Beethoven wrote a symphony in praise of it. Joy, heavenly joy, is perhaps the fulcrum of the universe. The nearer we are to God, the more we are filled with joy. To be cast out, to be far from the center of things, means to be far from joy. Cheerfulness and gaiety are two of the faces of joy, a gift of grace, something inexplicably wonderful that can happen to us in the depths of sickness, deprivation, torment, and confinement. Martyrs have sung while their bodies were crushed and burnt and pierced. Joy surpasses happiness, love feeds it, goodness is its outcome. Pleasure is an intimation of joy, happiness an approximation of it, but real joy is incandescent, ineffable, a blinding transcendental bliss.

Reserve—

Defined in the dictionary as "reticence or silence." What we have in mind here is "reticence *and* silence," something for which English offers no term. The Germans have a word for it: *Verschwiegenheit*. (No language can express everything and we cannot think certain thoughts because our language does not provide words for them just as others cannot think certain thoughts, which we can entertain, because they do not speak English.) The "reserve," then, that we are thinking of consists of reticence and silence about projects we want to undertake. It is characteristic of people who achieve little or nothing that they *talk* so much of what they intend to do. Do it, but do not talk about it. Talk is the enemy of action.

Prudence

Is derived from the Latin *providentia*, or foresight. Prudence implies caution, wisdom, planning, looking into the future, assessing the consequences of our actions and omissions. The prudent person has imagination. If it gets the better of him, he will become anxious and discouraged, unable to act because he foresees disaster at every step. Yet prudence is better than rashness, caution better than temerity. We are not called to greatness; survival is enough. Prudence is not a heroic virtue, yet one needed by all of us. Necessary as it may be, prudence can also be an insidious and dangerous virtue, because it may make cowards of us all.

Meditation

Is indeed what this book is all about. What prayer was in times long past, meditation should be today. Prayer meant talking to God. Today, we may believe in the existence of God, but have difficulty believing in His direct intervention. Although not all of the relief and assurance that prayer once gave can be achieved today by meditation, much of it can. Also, we have nothing better. If, as the German Existentialist philosopher Karl Jaspers said, our life resembles a text written in cipher, it is our task to decode that text and get at its meaning. Calm thought, rich in associations, personal yet objective, poetical and sober at the same time, meditation in other words, is the key to that cipher. Meditation is what we can do from our side. Illumination may be given to us, but only by grace, not as a reward. Knocking at the door does not guarantee that it will be opened. But without knocking we have no chance at all.

Equanimity

Only in America does one find books with titles like: *Adventures in Cooking* or *The Thrill of Knitting*. Our language is hyperbolic, our mass entertainment—like that of ancient Rome—a stew of sex, sensation, and sadism. As our tongue seems to enlarge whatever emerges from our mouth, the press, radio, and television also exaggerate and sensationalize their material. Forty million children going to school without incident are no news, one child killed by a lunatic makes headlines and convinces 250 million Americans that lunatics lurk behind every tree. Equanimity is won by seeing all things in their proper perspective, including our own life.

Sentimentality—

A scare word, if ever there was one! Don't let yourself be intimidated by it. If somebody calls your feelings sentimental, call his observations snide. Feelings, after all, make us happy or unhappy; nothing else does. Live your emotions to the fullest–inside yourself. Love, hate, rage, adore, or despise–but refrain from any action or utterance engendered solely by your feelings, unless and until you have thoroughly examined them. At the very least, put a day and a night between emotion and action. Also, do not forget that men are subject to stronger and more violent feelings than women and that they are more prone to act rashly under the spur of an emotion. With these provisos go ahead and enjoy nostalgia, love, melancholy, all the sweet feelings of admiration and tenderness. Sentimentality seldom hurts, though it is boring when encountered in others. Like sex and digestion, feelings should be a private matter.

Heartiness—

All right, but no vulgarity! This is a fine line which all too many boisterous, back-slapping, hail-fellow-well-met boosters easily overstep. A person who feels inclined to be hearty, rollicking, frolicsome should be aware that he may alienate many who consider what he deems good fun to be incredible rudeness and vulgarity. The worst thing is false heartiness, emanating from people who are not exuberant at all, or who use heartiness as a sales gimmick. Heartiness is not a license for foul language, tasteless jokes, or thinly veiled aggression.

Regularity

Has acquired odd connotations of digestive periodicity through "delicate" advertising. This, of course, is not what we mean here. We are thinking of the Victorian "regular habits." Most creative persons adhere to rigorous schedules. The great fundamental inspiration may come in a blinding flash, unbidden and unexpectedly, but the many small inspirations that are needed to complete a major work come only on schedule, like trains. Thomas Mann had such a regular regime of writing, correcting, and relaxing that his wife did not dare to interrupt him even with the news that war had broken out. In admiring a great work of art, literature, or scientific discovery, we are always apt to forget the immense industry, patience, and strict regularity which were needed to finish it.

Elegance—

A graceful perfection in actions, things, and people. We do not speak here of the elegance which consists of being fashionable. What we have in mind is rather that quality which mathematicians refer to when they speak of an elegant proof. When the trained singer performs seemingly without effort, when the acrobat does his stunts as if they were child's play, when the balls seem to return to the juggler's hand by themselves, then we have that true elegance which is always the end product of years of effort and training. Elegance arises where the effort it took to achieve it has become invisible. Art needs its audience and so does elegance.

Advice

Except in cases of dire emergency such as imminent suicide, crime, or accident, advice should never be given, unless specifically and repeatedly requested. Never give advice in matters of money, marriage, health, or law. Referral to competent authority is usually the best advice anyway. Never recommend or suggest a course of action. Let him who seeks your advice explain his problem so thoroughly and so often that the right course of action becomes evident by itself. Let him find the solution, but help by showing a multiplicity of options and opportunities and helping him to visualize the consequences of his actions. Do not interfere in the lives of others unless your calling as parent, teacher, priest, doctor, or lawyer forces you to do so.

Criticism

Should, like advice, only be offered when asked or paid for, i.e., professionally tendered. However tempting, never be blunt, epigrammatic, slashing, or stunning in criticism. It will get you laughter, but also enmity. All criticism should be sober, tactful, clothed in inoffensive, even soothing language. Dwell on any positive aspects you can find. Make allowances. Clearly state your competence to judge or any lack thereof. Whether there is such a thing as "constructive criticism" must be doubted. Constructive criticism would include propositions of how to do it differently and better, but then that would be good advice, reconstruction, new creation, and no longer criticism.

Hypocrisy

In small doses lubricates human interaction. I ought to smile, though I may instinctively dislike a person on first meeting him or her. I ought to say, "How are you?" though I could not care less. As a man I must assume that women are fragile, high-minded, and every so often helpless human beings, which of course they are not. Some mothers simply must pretend to love their children, though they may loathe them or be completely indifferent to them. Integrity fanatically observed makes us unfit for human society, in which case the absurdly untruthful person has indeed no other choice but to exile himself into the wilderness, there to talk to plants and animals. The rest of us cannot get along with each other without a touch of hypocrisy.

Absurdity

Is the nutrient on which imagination, humor, invention, delight, and surprise grow. I knew a professor who had a kitchen sink in his office. The sink was absurd, but it was also oddly useful and appealing. When it was removed, he and his colleagues felt a keen sense of loss. The absurd is fun only when it is not contrived. (The kitchen sink in our paradigm had been institutionally inherited, not requested.) Men and women with a sense for the absurd are good company, because they will always be tolerant. The acceptance of the absurd may be an outgrowth of resignation; the relish of and joy felt in absurdity, however, are signs of sturdy vitality and high good humor.

Naiveté

As an acquired trait or pretense is probably as difficult to achieve as naturalness. Naiveté is harmless ignorance or ignorant harmlessness, a childlike trust in the goodness of others, a lack of worldly knowledge. Children alone can be truly naive . . . and even there, beware! Naiveté was thought to be a desirable trait in young ladies of the Victorian age and one of the dread specters of that age was the elderly lady who still pretended to be naive, innocent, unspoiled. One may doubt that real naiveté in any form still exists, should or can still exist, even, in this age. Our task, whether we like it or not, is to become fully conscious. The point about true naiveté, however, was that it was entirely unconscious, precisely naive, not knowing, sweetly innocent, and touchingly "simple."

Perspicacity

If applied to situations is simply a function of intelligence and careful observation; if applied to persons, a talent for looking behind the masks we all wear and indeed must wear if civilization is to continue. Perspicacity is a happy medium between suspicion—one can err because one is too "realistic"—and naive trust. Most of the motives of our own or other people's actions may be egotistical and base, but some are good, unselfish, even kind and loving. A perspicacious man is not only one who discovers a scoundrel, but also one who discovers a good and upright person. Perspicacity, linguistically, has something to do with "looking through," looking through the disguises we wear, the roles we play, the obfuscations, deceits, mimicries, and guile we practice.

Worry—

Or, if you like a term à la mode, *angst*, is an eminently healthy, normal, and human trait. Heidegger, in fact, saw *angst* as a constituent characteristic of our existence. Excessive worry, of course, is harmful, but so is everything else done or suffered in excess. In my experience the best way of coping with worry is to do it consciously, to worry out loud, to say to oneself: now I am worrying and while I am at it, I might as well do a good job of it. By conscious, directed, and intensive worry one gets over it most quickly. Worry becomes much more of a problem if one listens to foolish people who tell us not to worry. On the contrary: worry, if you feel like it, but worry wholeheartedly until worry disappears by itself.

Fear—

Anxiety and worry—the latter being anxiety in a minor key—are perfectly normal and necessary constituents of our mind without which we could not survive. They are warning systems that only become dangerous to us if unreasonable or excessive and to others if they lead to preemptive strikes and paranoia, i.e., insane or criminal aggression. The person who knows no fear or anxiety is either incredibly stupid or harbors a secret death wish. Professional risk takers like steeple jacks or pilots or race car drivers are not foolhardy. They are cautious and careful, fearful in other words, well aware of what could happen if things go wrong. In general one can trust one's fears. Not only should one not be ashamed of them, one should listen carefully to what they try to tell us.

Aging—

A difficult task for many people. In our civilization we usually err in trying to appear younger than we are, in other times and cultures the young sometimes appeared ridiculous because they adopted postures and habits (in both senses of the word) of persons much older. If the consequence of wrong aging would only be ridicule, no harm done. But all too often men and women develop deleterious feelings of inadequacy and inferiority because they no longer look or feel as young as they once did. Both sexes may go in for activities far too strenuous for them, to seek cures which will disappoint them. If you are old, do not fear ridicule but fear your own vanity because it may kill you before your time is up.

Concentration—

There are two kinds: one is willed and the other is not. Willed concentration is that which we need for problem solving, learning, sports, in dangerous and ticklish situations. The other kind—cleverly observable in little boys, in composers, mystics, mathematicians, philosophers, poets, and scientists—is the one that overcomes us in the act of creation. This kind of concentration, where one has a feeling of being gripped by another power, is lovely while it lasts. For the truly creative person creation is sheer pleasure; his or her difficulty is coping with life. The distraught professor is not distraught, he is too concentrated. Such creative people need understanding and helpful spouses or good institutions like monasteries or British colleges to shelter and protect them.

Routine—

The greatest blessing there is! The world does not suffer from too much but from too little routine. Regularity, reliability, and only slow, slow, slow change—or better yet, no change at all for a while—is what we need. History runs faster now than before, we cannot adjust quickly enough and we suffer from a lack of predictability. We think of routine always in terms of boredom or bureaucratic inflexibility when we should think of it as an orderly way of doing things, as a sustaining and constructive element in our lives.

Religion

Presupposes the existence of higher beings or essences to whom we are related by love or fear. Primitive religion is out to placate those divinities, to make them favorably disposed toward us, to crave their help or indulgence. More advanced religions usually eschew concepts of direct influence from our side, but rather think in terms of aligning ourselves with those higher beings, principles, spiritualities that may help us find out what God, Nature, Tao, or any other demiurge has in mind and to live accordingly. Religion, any religion, is a good thing provided it does not develop a missionary zeal. Be religious, but be it for yourself alone. None of us knows all the truth. As St. Paul said, "we know in part and we prophesy in part."

Strictness

Is a sort of moral backbone. It does not say anything about the things we are strict about, but attests only to the fact that whatever principles we may have, they are such that we "strictly" enforce them for ourselves and occasionally for our children, spouses, friends, associates, and other resident taxpayers. Strictness is a double-edged sword: harmless when applied to ourselves, doubtful already when applied to everybody. It is difficult to find the right medium between exaggerated strictness and excessive softness, especially in education and rehabilitation. At least, let us be aware of the pitfalls of either extreme.

Fairness

It is not quite true that other languages have no word for "fairness"; they have other, but ultimately equivalent terms or circumlocutions. (To draw moral conclusions from linguistic evidence is usually wrong—the Germans, Swiss, or Austrians are not wicked because they coined a term like *Schadenfreude*; we have an equivalent term: gloating.) Fairness means playing by the rules, having a sense of justice and equity, acknowledging another person's justified claims. Sometimes it means acknowledging these claims before they are put forward. It also means refraining from hasty judgment, giving the other fellow a chance to explain, considering all factors. Fairness may be a purely civic virtue, having little to do with charity, love, or mercy, but until all men are angels, fairness is the nearest thing to goodness.

Cleverness

Is in itself a neutral quality, yet it has acquired unpleasant connotations. It seems to bespeak an egoistical cunning, the adroit manipulation of men and circumstances, the capture of small advantages. All that may be true of many clever people, but on the other hand to be clever also means not to get lost in dreams and illusions, to be realistic, to keep one's eyes open, to be on guard and to act prudently, consciously, intentionally. Great saints have been practical and often clever. Goodness does not exclude cleverness. Certainly, not all clever people are good people, but then—neither are all stupid people good.

Beauty

What people worry about is the physical beauty one receives as a gift. They should worry about the beauty one creates or destroys. Is there a moral obligation to create or preserve beauty? Not in our civilization, unfortunately, though we pay lip service to the attributes of perfection: goodness, truth, and beauty. Beauty so far has been neglected, though there are now some signs that beauty—Apollonian beauty, of course, the beauty of order, health, nature, cleanliness, quiet, and sanity—is being considered as something that should be enforced, that is everybody's business, that should not be a privilege of the rich. As to the beauty one possesses: do not worry about it, even if you are a woman. Attractiveness is only to a small degree dependent upon physical beauty.

Independence—

The one and only reason to make and save more money than one needs, charity excepted. The strongest argument for a capitalist society—or better said for a society which recognizes and protects private property, since our Western societies are no longer truly capitalist—is that only in such a society can one reach a maximum of independence, hence of freedom. Where I am totally dependent upon others, may they be ever so well-meaning, I am ultimately dependent upon bureaucrats and administrators. In a capitalist society, however, sufficient money can reserve a space for me where organizational tyrants cannot enter. Too little money makes me dependent; moderate money protects me; too much money exposes me to terrorism, blackmail, envy, hatred, and a different kind of insecurity.

Credibility

The very fact that this is no longer used referring only to the truth of a tall story, but also attesting to the intent of government policies, financial undertakings of respectable banks, military threats, diplomatic interventions, and ransom demands bespeaks a frightening deterioration of public and private trust. Since no person or institution can be trusted anymore, image making has become an industry. Image making, masking, projection of that which is not so or not quite so is called advertising, public relations, political management, skillful presentation. Sad to say, an honest, unfeigning person is frequently no longer "credible," precisely because he or she scorns manipulation. Increasingly, it is no longer possible to be credible by simply being honest, upright, and sincere.

Health

Has become a moral issue. We are obliged to be healthy. Not to be healthy is no longer considered a punishment of the Lord, meted out in just retribution for some sin, but the natural consequence of some failure on our part. Illness is considered to be avoidable and people have a bad conscience when they are sick. Though much sickness is due to self-indulgence and carelessness, much of it is a result of fate—heredity and environment for instance—ignorance, or just plain bad luck. The preoccupation with health by itself can become unhealthy. Illness can have positive aspects. It may force us to re-assess our way of life, it may become spiritually productive, our own suffering may make us more sensitive to the sufferings of others. Pain is a cruel taskmaster. It may be utterly senseless, but it may also nudge us that little step nearer to perfection which we otherwise would not have taken.

Joie de vivre—

Or *Lebensfreude*, as the Germans have it. The joy of living is largely, though not absolutely, dependent upon good health. There is an element of abundance, overflowing, of dancing and singing in it, an expenditure of psychical and physical energy over and above that which is strictly necessary. Also, of course, an acknowledgment of the world as good and beautiful. People who have this joie de vivre are irresistible. Even if they are scoundrels, one loves them. They are always immensely attractive to the opposite sex. Nothing gets them down for long. They are never bored and always have the feeling, the conviction even, that they are lucky, that happiness is the normal state of mankind and that they are indeed God's favorite children.

Adventure

Is a narrow escape which can be told to others. If there is no reference to those in whose eyes the adventurer becomes a dashing hero, the adventure turns out to be a simple mishap, a foolish enterprise, a childish play with risk and danger. Let us suppose somebody went out to slay dragons and indeed fights them in dangerous and picturesque forays, but when he returns finds that all his contemporaries have died and that nobody is interested anymore in dragons, has not the original adventure then ceased to be one? Or even worse: let us suppose that while fighting dragons, our adventurer suddenly finds out that he can no longer go back, that henceforth he *must* fight dragons. End of adventure.

Rationality

Seems to be a dreary negative virtue, but is in reality our only defense against the forces of darkness, confusion, passion, and crime. There is love, to be sure, but love can be blind. Love can be a great spoiler, unless it is paired with reason, although rationality is more than being reasonable. Rationality means to develop thinking, planning, consciousness, and control. But does this not have a desiccating effect in the long run? Does this not exclude poetry, beauty, aesthetic enjoyment, and artistic endeavor? Not at all—it is precisely as rational human beings that we must understand our need for occasional excursions into the realms of art and play, those areas which are free of specific aims and uses, not goal-directed, not competitive, not exploitative, but given to pure enjoyment, to dreaming and feeling.

Intensity

There's an old cartoon in *Punch* where an aesthetic young lady asks a stolid young man: "Are you intense?" A mysterious quality—this intensity. It may have something to do with above average nervous energy, with greater stamina and stronger concentration. Intensity is the great ideal of all young people. Can it be acquired? Scarcely. No amount of good intention will convert a low-voltage person into a high-voltage one. Less intense people generally admire those who are more so. "Only love defends us against great qualities in another person," said Goethe. However admirable—and occasionally irritating—intense people are, the world needs also contemplative, calm, and nonaggressive persons. Sloths and snails are as necessary as ants and squirrels.

Bravery

Is the outcome of courage. Courage wills, bravery does. Bismarck spoke of "civil courage." Risking one's life, the heroism of policemen, fire fighters, soldiers, sailors, and pilots is the bravery of military courage. Too much bravery can become provocation, temerity, and irresponsible daring, not bravery but bravado. Still, bravery is one of the greatest human virtues. He who has it is worth our love and admiration. Yet bravery, oddly enough, is sporadic and selective: a bullfighter may be superstitious, a much decorated general may stand in mortal fear of his dentist, a man may climb Mount Everest and be afraid of a spider. Be not afraid or ashamed of your fears. Civil courage is rarer than bravery and none of us is always and totally brave.

Talk

Is perhaps what life is all about. We talk incessantly, silently to ourselves, aloud to others. Thinking is inward talking, except for cerebral activities such as musical composition or recall. Nearly all the influence we exert on others or power we have over them, comes through talk. Next to reading, it is our prime source of information, which women seem to know better than men. In fact, we need talk. The horrors of non-talk are vividly experienced in solitary confinement or in the "cold shoulder" of certain unions or prisons. The aim of all social gatherings is talk. If we get irritated with talk, it is because it may be abused, become trivial and bore us. Good talk nourishes the soul, brightens the mind, and renders us happy and content.

Chivalry—

The virtue of the man on horseback, an eminently masculine and aristocratic virtue, presupposing the existence of a code of honor and of a stratified, nonegalitarian society in which those "above" feel a strong obligation to those "below," the medieval society in other words in its ideal form. It was the duty of the knight to protect the weak and helpless, women and children, widows and orphans, the old and infirm—a noble ideal every so often realized. Even in its latest and attenuated forms as gallantry or courtesy or generosity, good form and fair play are still a valid postulate. *Noblesse oblige*. We try to cope with the body politic by written constitutions and contractual obligations; other times relied on loyalty, tradition, feelings, and enthusiasms. Genuine chivalry can no longer exist, because we no longer believe in the possibility of existential superiority. If all men are equal, none can be superior.

Seriousness

Does not preclude joyfulness and gaiety. As a positive quality it is the opposite of fickleness and superficiality. A man who lacks seriousness is shallow, flippant, vain, and trifling; his female counterpart is silly, giddy, empty-headed. A man who cannot take anything seriously either poses or is deranged, usually the former because there will always be one person whom he takes seriously: himself. Seriousness, in the aftermath of the Victorian age, has too often been confused with pedantry and surliness. A serious person is simply one who makes a distinction between important and unimportant matters, has an aim, lives for a purpose. There are many things which are serious and important and the manner in which we deal with them is the measure of our existential size.

Creativity

Has too exclusively been seen as only a sublimation of sexuality, especially in the case of women. "Since she does not (or cannot) have babies, she writes books." It is not that simple. Some highly sexed people have had both: children and creativity (Bernini, Bach, George Sand, Clara Schumann), others had little or no sex life (Fra Angelico, Handel) and still created many works. In our opinion, creativity depends upon an initial energy push with which each person is born. One may be able to dissipate much of it, but one probably cannot do much to enlarge or to intensify it. If this entelechy, this *a priori* existing energy quantum is large, it will provide for both biological and intellectual, artistic, or spiritual creativity. If it is small, it will only suffice for either sex or creativity. Sex is not transmuted into creativity; both sex and creativity stem from the same source.

Delicacy

Has a double aspect: physical and spiritual. Physical delicacy may greatly contribute to spiritual perfection, compassion, even creativity. One thinks of Proust, Chopin, and Elizabeth Barrett Browning. Delicacy, however, in its spiritual aspect involves empathy, the ability to anticipate and to experience in imagination the feelings of others. As Americans we are not much given to delicacy and out of our Puritan and pioneer heritage rather prize toughness, activity, and robust strength. Oddly enough, most progress comes from the delicate, sensitive, and vulnerable people. They do not and cannot effect change, but they are the ones who become sensitive to the sufferings of others, to moral shortcomings, to callousness, cruelty, brutality, and exploitation. They are the ones who initiate change and upward movement.

It is the power that is mighty in the weak.

Repetition—

M*ater est studiorum*—the mother of studies—one learns by repetition. No author can avoid repetition. It is an indispensable element of music. We fear repetition, because it may produce boredom, satiety, aversion. Yet the moment we think of repetition in terms of rhythm, regularity, recurrence, it loses its horror. We live only as long as our hearts and lungs monotonously repeat their task. Repetition, far from being deadly, is the *sine qua non* of human and cosmic existence and those who are wise in the ways of the spirit know that great and beneficial forces lie in the repetition of sacred prayers, formulae, mantras, liturgies, and incantations. Novelty, variety, and incessant change are not always good for us. The world needs more preservers than reformers.

Perfection

Be ye perfect as our Father in Heaven is perfect, says the Bible. What is meant is religious, spiritual, moral perfection. We shall never achieve perfection, but we should strive for it. Or should we rather not? Perfectionism may be a form of insidious pride. "I demand perfection from myself and for myself, because I am more than others. They may be imperfect, I must be perfect." Who does not know the mother and wife who drives her family to despair with her fussiness, or the boss who can never be satisfied, or the artist who rarely produces anything because nothing is perfect enough? Striving after perfection leads to human greatness and glory only where it is imbued with a profound and sincere humility. Also: she who bakes a perfect cake has achieved more than he who has invented another, necessarily imperfect, scheme for saving the world.

Compassion—

The virtue of saints and the acme of moral perfection. What distinguished the founders of the world's great religions more than anything else was compassion, the ability, indeed the compulsion, to suffer with those who suffer, to feel the pain of others, to share their sorrow, grief, and hurt. Love which is not compassionate is simply desire, not love. Though it is already an achievement to feel compassion—a feeling of which the wicked and insane are bereft—true compassion does not end there; it always proceeds to deeds of helping, healing, consoling, and comforting. Compassion is the purest form of love.

Moderation

May be the virtue of Philistines and of the old and infirm. But Philistines in general live normal, uneventful, healthy, long, and happy lives, and even the old and infirm who practice moderation not because they want to but because they have to are better off for it. Moderation may not lead to victory and success, but it helps us to survive. The Greeks thought highly of moderation—which proves that they themselves were given to passion and excess. Moderation is most admirable where it keeps a strong vitality within bounds. For him in whom vitality is not a torrent but a trickle, it is easy to be moderate. The lack of moderation may make life adventurous, dynamic, and flamboyant, but it may also lead to madness, disgrace, sickness, and early death.

Interest

Is not something inherent in persons, things, or happenings, but is a disposition in which the mind is allowed to be attracted to and entertained by something other than oneself. Though it has been said that anything and everything becomes interesting if looked at long enough, I would say that persons, things, or events which utterly repel us cannot become interesting because we cannot bring ourselves to look at them and that the looking itself must be of a special kind, a bit scientific as it were, speculative and exploring. Persons who find nearly everything interesting, who are never bored, who are always delighted, surprised, entertained are usually those who are articulate, observant, relating easily to others, and totally absorbed in the world around them. The world becomes interesting in the measure to which we can forget ourselves.

Exclusiveness

Is perfectly justified, acceptable, and under certain circumstances even good and necessary. Not everybody can or should be our friend. We have a right to choose our friends. Exclusiveness is morally and legally wrong where it deprives qualified people of access to work and education, to pay and promotion, to equal protection under the law, and to all those services and facilities which are in the public domain. Yet if some red-headed Irishmen want to found a club of their own and thus exclude all women, all other Irishmen, all minorities and majorities, all other races and nations except red-headed Irishmen, they have a perfect right to do so. Freedom is also the freedom to exclude.

Dialogue—

Our thinking is a constant dialogue with ourselves. (Who or what speaks to whom or which is still a mystery.) Our inner dialogue is as important as the dialogue with others. One supports the other. Active, energetic, and creative people maintain not only that inner dialogue which is the source of their ideas, inventions, and inspirations, they usually can talk to others and enjoy doing so. Where dialogue ceases, we are diminished. True dialogue, where one party also listens to the other, is very rare. Television is not good for us, because others do their talking for us. We ought to talk to each other or to ourselves. In that sense reading (as a conversation with an author) is good, but real conversation is better. Here as elsewhere: giving is better than receiving. Genuine dialogue is impossible where propaganda and persuasion rear their ugly heads.

Discernment

Is very much needed in a world which batters our minds with advertising, propaganda, slanted news, and exaggerations or deceives us by not giving the whole picture, by omission and distortion. We must read between the lines. We must, unfortunately, distrust anything and everything that we hear over the air, see on TV, or read in a newspaper, book, or magazine. We are being manipulated day in, day out, virtually every waking hour of the day and not only freely and openly with our knowledge and consent as in church or school or in the doctor's office, but slyly, insidiously, often subconsciously, and certainly without our knowledge and consent. Discernment is not a sufficient but a necessary condition of our freedom.

Flexibility—

Or, as current usage has it, keeping one's options open. Flexibility is one of those ambiguous virtues which easily becomes a vice. Certainly, adaptability and resourcefulness, originality and quickness in finding a way out of an impasse are admirable qualities. Where flexibility refers to moral issues, however, such as bending the law, taking the easiest and sleaziest way out, waving in any wind, it is abominable. Lack of conscience, courage, and conviction are often covered by the pretense of flexibility. While "high morals" and "lofty ideals" were the hypocrisies of yore, flexibility is the hypocrisy of our age. There is something to be said for "situation ethics," but not much.

Service

"*Ich dien,*" the motto of the Prince of Wales: I serve. As José Ortega y Gasset pointed out in his delightful book *Invertebrate Spain*, service was once not only honorable and exciting, it was the only way to advancement and personal fulfillment. It is only in modern times where service is no longer a gift, but a contractual obligation expressed in terms of cash value, that service is being rendered indifferently and in most cases with the firm intention of giving a minimum of service for a maximum of pay. The reward of service should be joy and satisfaction, not money alone. Service, alas, has become a commodity reluctantly traded, greatly devalued, and ridiculously overpraised in greedy advertising.

Representation

Is the fiction by which large democracies like ours exist. A true democracy is, of course, only a direct one like Switzerland or ancient Greece. Nobody can truly "represent" thousands of different people. Any representative first and foremost represents himself. We have to abide by "democratic" conventions for lack of better. They are neither efficient nor rational, but we do not have any other which we could accept. By extension, self-representation is our mask, the persona we have chosen and elaborated over the years, our visible character. There is nothing wrong with "putting one's best foot forward." One should not be vain, foppish, posturing, and ridiculous, but neither should one be rude and repulsive. We should appear as better than we are, but that appearance must become a second nature. Our appearance is the flag thrown amongst the enemy and thence
to be recovered.

Sweetness

Though Pindar in his odes spoke of the sweetness that is in men, we think of it as an essentially feminine trait. Only small boys or old men are allowed to be sweet. Otherwise we have to speak of masculine affability, bonhomie, courtesy, or good nature. Sweetness in women, however, is not only permitted, it is highly praised and consists of that smiling compliance, that indulgence, that anticipation of another person's wishes, that tenderness, softness, and apparent humility by which women rule the world. Actually, women can be tough as nails and in our civilization usually prevail. Where sweetness is genuine, it is one of the loveliest and most powerful forces, virtually irresistible. Venus is a great goddess, adorable and fearsome.

Simplicity

Often becomes affectation. One tries to avoid ostentation and ends up with the pretense of simplicity which can be worse than a moderate amount of social ritual. *A priori*, simplicity is not preferable to complication, subtlety, multiplicity, and intricacy. In the categories of our thinking there is one which urges us toward elaboration and another one which demands simplification. The simplicity of any solution does not argue for its rightness, just as the truth in any given case may or may not be simple. Simplicity as the avoidance of affectation is good. Simplicity as a pretext for the avoidance of deeper thought, more careful attention, and better behavior is bad. Good manners are more important than rude simplicity.

Respect

Was once thought to be the hallmark of a noble and well brought up person. We have lost respect for respect. In fact, every so often we laud the absence of respect, as if respect had always been a tribute to sham and wickedness. Not so: there were times when respect shown to hallowed institutions and sacred persons, to superior rank or knowledge, to moral excellence, to wisdom, to old age, to goodness or refinement, to genius or even talent exalted not only the institution or person to which respect was shown, but also the respectful person himself. Respect makes both parties happy. It is the acknowledgment of superiority which is always easily and gladly rendered by persons who are a bit superior themselves.

Energy

God, how one envies those who have it! Energy is a function of health, genetic endowment, cultural conditioning, climate, food, social circumstances, and so on. Energy does not exist in a vacuum. It differs from activity insofar as it not only spurs to action, but also overcomes resistance. If activity is like water, energy is like compressed steam. One must learn to husband one's energy. (Long distance runners do not go all out at the beginning.) Unless energy is coupled with patience and perseverance, it does not accomplish much. Short bursts of high-voltage energy are like lightning—brief, beautiful, destructive, and useless. What we all need is low-voltage but long-term energy, enduring warmth and steady glow.

Contemporaneity

Has a double aspect: to be one's age and to be of one's age. To be contemporaneous to one's own age is, if course, only important at and after middle age, because the young are always of their age. (There have been times, though, when the young tried to appear older than they were.) Today it is rather the older person who puts on the airs of youth and thus becomes ridiculous. "*Il faut être de son temps,*" said Honoré Daumier, the nineteenth-century French caricaturist and painter—one has to be of one's (historical) time. Yes and no—to be modern, to run with the crowd, to believe in all the latest fads and crazes, is not always right. There is nothing wrong with being conservative, even old-fashioned. Both kinds of contemporaneity require some thought and, under certain circumstances, some friendly advice from others.

Grooming

Does not, of course, bespeak any person's moral perfection. There may have been saints who were pigs. Beethoven, Brahms, van Gogh, and Frederick the Great were at times less than appetizing. Good grooming falls under the heading of *Weltklugheit*—worldly wisdom. Not everybody can be fashionable and elegant, but everybody can be clean, neat, and well groomed. Money spent on one's appearance and neat dress is always money well spent. We are judged by the way we look. A slob affronts our sensibilities, a slattern revolts us. The young and beautiful are forgiven some lapses in good grooming, but not the mature and elderly. We should not look repulsive or ridiculous and we should not sell ourselves too cheaply for want of a little attention to our appearance.

Conviction

Makes convicts of those who are convinced. We ought to have some convictions but allow flexibility, as there is nary a conviction which could not be superseded by a better one. A man or woman who, at the age of sixty, has the same convictions as at sixteen is probably stupid, insensitive, or insane. New facts and new circumstances will topple the deepest and most cherished convictions. How many sacrosanct and seemingly eternal convictions have not been upset by the arrival of the Pill! We should stand up for what we believe is right, but we should also admit the possibility that our beliefs may be wrong. Holy skepticism, be thou with us forever!

Commitment—

Too much of it leads to fanaticism, too little to weakness, frivolity, and emptiness. We are defined by our commitments or the lack thereof. The point is not so much what we are committed to as the depth and seriousness of that commitment. *Sub specie aeternitatis:* it matters little whether I die for this country or that country, for this religion or that religion, for this conviction or that. What matters is the sincerity and thought with which I choose my commitment and the strength with which I uphold it. Nietzsche said that dying for a conviction does not make it a right or even good conviction. Indeed not, but dying for any conviction makes a man a hero or martyr or saint. Where commitments are weak and insincere or absent altogether, a civilization has come to its end.

Roots

Are good if you have them and no disaster if you don't. What we inherit from them is our linguistic, intellectual, emotional, spiritual, and aesthetic constitution. Schiller's word: What you inherited from your fathers, acquire it in order to possess it, is right indeed, since he understood that inheritance to be our spiritual and cultural heritage. There were times when mankind lived in small, inbred, racially homogeneous groups. There intellectual and spiritual qualities may possibly have been transmitted through the bloodstream. No longer. Our task is to deepen, strengthen, and preserve our cultural heritage. This requires conscious effort, education, discipline.

Objectivity

Is, of course, impossible. Nobody can be objective and nobody ever was or is. We are all primed and prejudiced. Even the most objective reporter is subjective through his choice of items to report, through the use of an old language in which every word is loaded with emotional associations and through his own biography. Since our judgment can never be truly objective—who is there even to assess true objectivity?—we can do no more than be aware of our subjectivity and through the use of patient reasoning arrive at as objective a view as is humanly possible. Also: don't ever forget that you never know all the facts. A firm, assured, and categorical judgment is usually the judgment of a firm, assured, and categorical fool.

Parapsychology

Is a rather flat term denoting such phenomena as telepathy, telekinesis, clairvoyance, precognition, retrocognition, and magnetic healing which depend upon mysterious and as yet imperfectly understood paranormal faculties that possibly all of us possess to various degrees. If one is blessed—or cursed—with any of these supersensory faculties, one ought neither to foster nor to deny them. Any contact with higher worlds and thus also with lower worlds is fraught with danger. These powers are safe only if used totally selflessly, not for gain, not for power, not even for the satisfaction of scientific inquiry, but only and alone to help our fellow men. Rejoice if you are "normal"—and thus protected—be humble and loving, if you are "sensitive."

Coping

Starts with the firm conviction that every problem is solvable, that it is only a question of time and effort, of patience and intelligence to come up with an answer. Some people can cope with any and every difficulty, others are baffled and checked by the smallest unforeseen circumstance: Coping involves intelligence, flexibility, good nerves, good humor, optimism, and decision. Courage is of the essence and people who rightly or wrongly believe God (or His equivalent) is on their side will probably be better able to cope than those who feel helpless and abandoned. Know that every problem admits of several solutions. Avoid the company of those who cannot cope, unless you are a doctor, priest, or social worker. And do not forget that sleep and rest, love for others, interest in the world, and prayer are sovereign helpers in times of stress and sorrow.

Giving

We receive by giving. Love, gratitude, friendship—all the spiritual and emotional qualities which make life not only bearable but even enjoyable are enhanced, though not guaranteed, by giving. Selfish persons condemn themselves to loneliness, despair, sometimes even madness. Yet there is one condition to all giving: whatever is given must be given outright, without thought of recompense, requital, gratitude, or even acknowledgment. Giving for the sake of an advantage does not bring spiritual benefits; on the contrary, it will invariably lead to disappointment. Parents who love their children will be disappointed if they expect love in return. It may happen, but if so, then as a gift, not a reward. The joy of giving lies in the giving.

Naturalness

There is no such thing as perfect naturalness. Even the most primitive savage—and he probably more so than civilized man—is already "unnatural," culturally conditioned and acting "artificially." If we had neither brain nor individuality, we could be natural. What we mean when we praise naturalness is the absence of artifice, pretense, sham, and pomposity. Yet there is that fine line between behavior which is stilted and false, and that which is oafish and rude. Naturalness lies between those extremes, is difficult to achieve and in general a product of high civilization. One must learn to be natural, to be unselfconscious and spontaneous. Every actor knows that naturalness comes hardest. To be natural one must be convinced of one's own value and rectitude, because a perfectly natural person may also be a perfectly unpleasant beast or bore.

Intellect

Our nation enjoys the sad distinction of having coined the term "egghead." We are the only nation where words like "professor" or "intellectual" can be used as terms of opprobrium, where gifted children have a hard time at school, because they frighten both teachers and parents. We profess to love the man of action and pay enormous sums to those who by cunning and agility use the fruits of purely intellectual endeavor. Yet where would we be without our intellectuals? Intelligence is our most precious possession both collectively and individually. We dominate our world and ourselves by intelligence and we do not need less but more of it today and in times to come. We must have intellectuals however annoying their antics may be, however unpleasant their probing and questioning.

Intelligence

Makes for success and happiness, though through enhanced sensitivity, sharper observation, and greater awareness it may also cause pain and concern. Yet no other means—except perhaps blind faith—has been found with which to cope successfully with life's problems. The power of the intellect is awesome. None of us can comprehend and hold more than a tiny particle of the immense universe of human knowledge, aside from the fact that we can only think within the limits of our own language. Can intelligence be fostered? Of course it can; partly by correct food, physical exercise, hygiene, but mostly by parental interest, solid and demanding instruction, relentless intellectual exercise, and unstinting recognition of intellectual achievement.

Form

Is not formality, though good form probably will always comprise some formal behavior. Good form is rather the realization of a stylized behavior; in fact, form and style in this context are synonymous. The Germans speak of *Haltung* there, the French of *la tenue*. We really have no word for what is meant here, since the anti-aristocratic bias of Americans forbids them to admire good form. Yet they recognize it when they see it. Katharine Hepburn had it, John Kennedy and his wife in her younger years, Grace Kelly, Giscard d'Estaing, Talleyrand, and Lord Mountbatten. Form is a higher nature which has been acquired. Those who have it are often felt to be charismatic. More people had it or aspired to it in the past than today. Good form flourishes in hierarchies. It needs an admiring public, because it is role-playing of a high order.

Attractiveness—

Wrongly called charisma—is that mysterious power which Goethe called "demonic." Some people have it by nature, others must acquire it. It has little or nothing to do with physical beauty; neither Socrates nor Napoleon were handsome, nor for that matter were Sarah Bernhardt or Alma Mahler-Werfel-Gropius. What makes a person attractive is among other things his or her ability to make others feel important, intelligent, handsome, and interesting. To become attractive one must take care not to be self-centered or negative. In social contexts, an attractive person is able to forget himself and concentrate on the other person. (Genuinely so! False attention means grimacing and is always transparent.) The good actor thinks of his public, not of himself, the good teacher thinks of his student, the attractive person of those with whom he or she interacts.

Charisma

Should not be used as a synonym for charm, attractiveness, or persuasive power. Charisma, until recently, meant something like divine grace bestowed upon a person by which he or she could bring spiritual blessings—and sometimes physical healing—to others. True charisma is the attribute of saints and saintly leaders: Gandhi had it and Joan of Arc, St. Francis and John Wesley. Charisma is entirely a gift from above. It can be given to those who strive for it and to those who are surprised by it. Most of us have never met a truly charismatic personality, but when we do, it is usually a soul-shaking experience. A saint makes us feel very small, not through his preaching, but through his being.

Aestheticism

There is nothing wrong with a sense of beauty, though our civilization concedes it only to women. There have been aesthetic civilizations which were thoroughly masculine: medieval Persia, old Japan, ancient Greece. We always think of an aesthete as an effeminate, ridiculous Oscar Wilde type of man, though we cannot praise feminine aestheticism highly enough. We allow artists and actors, interior decorators and dress designers, dancers and poets a measure of aestheticism and we have staked out certain areas like gardening or stamp collecting where a man can indulge in aesthetic pleasure. Note that aestheticism is ethically neutral, a matter of taste and preference.

Strength—

The word covers a multitude of virtues and qualities. Physical strength is essentially a gift of Nature. In spite of advertising and manly exhortation: exercise, diet, hygiene, and sober living will only develop that potential which was given us through heredity. We cannot acquire physical strength beyond the limitations of our natural endowment. It is different with moral and spiritual strength; in fact, cripples and weaklings have often exhibited an astounding tenacity and courage. Human will and determination can achieve miracles of moral, intellectual, and spiritual strength. That kind of strength is most often, but not always, developed by those whose being is centered in a mission, a sacred conviction, sometimes a fanaticism, but always in some being or cause outside, above or beyond themselves.

Vigor

Is not an always accessible resource. Even the most vigorous person cannot be vigorous at all times. Even Teddy Roosevelt must have had his moments of weakness and discouragement, of lassitude and exhaustion. Yet a certain measure of vigor is within the reach of all of us, if we but heed a few simple precepts: Get involved! Get involved with people, animals, plants, books, studies, sports, hobbies, charity—whatever. Shun too much passivity, e.g., television. See a doctor, if you are constantly tired (see several doctors!), study nutrition, try out yoga, t'ai chi, ballet, aerobics, or any other system of gymnastics. Get away from the standard American diet of sugar, soft drinks, white bread, and canned food. Do not smoke, drink, or take drugs! Sleep enough! Walk! Be as much in and under natural light as possible! (If female: wear sensible shoes.) And, most important of all, give and accept love!

Attention

Is an important favor which we can freely bestow or withhold. All of us want and need attention, except a few saints (who want the attention of God). Fame, glory, recognition are but conspicuous forms of attention. Children crave attention. So does everybody else down to the lowest criminal—who may, in fact, have become a criminal because that modicum of attention any human being needs was not given to him or her. In Belgium which, I think, was the first nation to abolish capital punishment, the "silent" treatment of total non-attention given to some prisoners is so hard to bear that flinty criminals have begged to be executed. Attention is the soul of courtesy. Real or assumed indifference may hurt more than open hatred. Great men and women have always been exquisitely attentive to the joys and griefs, the needs and wishes, the moods and opinions of others.

Gallantry—

The altruism of the strong—meant originally what Webster's says it means, namely "spirited and conspicuous bravery." Later on it became identified, especially in the adjective "gallant," with a specific chivalrous attitude toward women. This gallantry always assumed that women, because they were beings of a different and definitely higher order, had to be protected by men. Emancipated women have at all times rejected both assumptions. We reserve judgment, but beg to point out that any man in the interest of domestic peace, of his success with the other sex, and more and more even in the interest of his own career, does well to abide stubbornly by both assumptions. As it is, gallantry may well be the last refuge of male dominance.

Worship

While a phrase like "I adore ice cream" is bad, "I worship ice cream" is even worse, because worship implies a deeper commitment than adoration. Worship *per se* is good, as long as there is no fanaticism, no missionary activity, no conversion of others by thought control, brainwashing, intimidation, or political and economic pressure involved. Does it matter whom or what one worships or is reverence alone enough? Is a phrase like "worshipping money" justified? Can one hypostatize health, wealth, or power into divinities? One thing is sure (and Christ said so already): let your worship be as private as possible. Mankind has waded through rivers of blood because the people and their leaders could not agree on whom or what, when and how to worship. Worship nourishes the soul, but sometimes starves the brain.

Poverty—

If voluntary—may be a virtue, Rilke's *grosser Glanz von innen*, a great splendor from within. Involuntary poverty is usually resented, though opinions vary widely as to what constitutes poverty. In America a man is poor if he does not have running hot water and electricity. We take food, clothes, and shelter for granted. Poverty does not exclude happiness. People make us happy, not things. Poverty is terrible where it brings slavery, repression, exploitation, ill health, overwork, and early death. It is terrible where it limits freedom, stunts intellectual and physical growth, breeds crime and insanity. Yet some of the poorest people on earth are happy, healthy, and content. The abolition of poverty is highly desirable, but it will not make man happier, wiser, or better.

vigilance

Forewarned: forearmed. What distinguishes vigilance from alertness? One is alert to suddenly appearing, quickly passing phenomena; one is vigilant in a calmer, more consistent and lasting way for a long time. To be vigilant in a moral sense means to be on guard, to foresee difficulties, to evade temptations, to exercise self-control. Should we be vigilant for others too? Am I my brother's keeper? Yes, we should stand up for our convictions where we do so out of love and concern. But let us temper vigilance with tolerance. It is all too easy to persuade ourselves wherever and whenever we want to interfere, to condemn and to exclude, that we do so out of love and concern. One part vigilance over others must always be compensated for by nine parts vigilance over ourselves.

Warmth—

One has it or one does not have it. Some people are naturally effusive, extroverted, open-hearted, and open-handed; others are equally naturally cool, aloof, secretive, and reserved. Worldly wisdom is with the latter, worldly love, laughter, and joy with the former. Though our reason may ever so often say: keep out, stay away, be careful, our heart may urge us to help, to smile, to stretch out a hand, to be the first to greet or to apologize. One should not deny one's heart. Every human contact is risky. We may lose as much by too great a reserve as by too much affection. To be sure, there is always the danger that the good Samaritan will fall into a trap, that the person whom one helps will turn out to be ungrateful, wicked, and murderous, but there is an equal danger that the victim will die unless the good Samaritan helps him promptly.

Exercise—

Meaning physical exercise—has been greatly overvalued. Athletes die like other people, do not live longer—in fact, may die earlier *because* of exercise—and on the whole are neither happier nor healthier than others. They may feel better, though (and certainly superior), and may indeed enjoy a number of short-term advantages, such as better sleep or normal weight. Yet the exercise which counts is mental. However virtuous it may seem to stretch one's muscles, it is more important to stretch one's mind, to flex the muscles of one's soul, to gain in grace before God and men. All physical exercise must be strictly subordinate to other values. There is some merit in a healthy body, there is more in a healthy mind. Many beasts in human form enjoy the most remarkable good health. Exercise should be no more important in one's life than intestinal regularity or clean fingernails.

Friendliness

Costs so little and brings in such large rewards! It does not matter whether your friendliness is sincere or not: a little hypocrisy oils the wheels of any social machinery. If we brutally and frankly display our likes and dislikes, we are like children in a nursery who usually have a hard time getting along with each other because they are so frank and open. A bit of dissembling—call it self-control if you will—is absolutely necessary. Do not forget the old adage that a spoonful of honey attracts more bees than a bucket of vinegar. And, finally, lots of friendliness may bring little friendliness in return, but a tiny bit of unfriendliness may result in torrents of hostility.

Persuasion

Is the better part of force. To be sure, we want to bend another man's will to our own ends in either case, but force leaves wounds, resentment, hostility, and most of the time produces antagonism and counter-force, while persuasion may even make an enemy our friend and ally. Never threaten anybody. Always try to show him or her that what you want is in their own interest. If persuasion fails the first time, think up another argument and try again. And again. And again. If all else fails, either give up convincing the other person or—very carefully, slowly, and reluctantly—use force, but weigh the risks. The use of force may backfire. Do not go to court, except as the last, desperate, and virtually suicidal resort. Let calm and patient persuasion be your weapon. Be content with compromises.

Travel—

And travel while you are young! Soon enough you will be old and either unable or unwilling to travel. We are all provincials and commonly know only one country, one language, one culture. Travel is a virtue. It may even be a pleasure, though it usually is not much of a pleasure if one has to travel as a salesman for instance, or an engineer, or a soldier. One travels in order to store up impressions to meditate upon, to enlarge one's aesthetic and psychological perceptions, to enhance one's awareness. It does not matter whether one travels luxuriously or primitively, alone or in a group. A real penetration and understanding of another civilization cannot be achieved by travel anyhow, but only by prolonged residency. Travel does not so much instruct as stimulate. It is our reaction to the stimulus, our creative response to it which counts.

Self-knowledge—

As the Greeks knew very well—is indeed the beginning of all wisdom and the precondition of all higher knowledge. English has no precise equivalent for the German *Selbsterkenntnis* which we have in mind here. The eminently practical and earthy character of English rejects perhaps that introspection, that incipient schizophrenia which self-knowledge demands. One is supposed to look upon oneself as upon a stranger. Total self-knowledge thus is difficult, if not impossible. Meeting ourselves is always a searing experience and we shy away from it. Even outwardly seeing ourselves televised or hearing our voice on tape is already shocking. How much more so meeting ourselves psychologically and recognizing the weakness, meanness, and depravity of our character. Yet we cannot progress unless we confront ourselves in this type of inspection.

Curiosity

Killed the cat. Maybe, but it also saved it on innumerable other occasions. Women, it is said, are more curious than men. If so, it would speak for their higher intelligence. Yet I believe that the curiosity of women is more directed toward persons, while that of men is directed toward objects and issues. Curiosity itself is morally neutral. It becomes obnoxious, if it interferes with the lives of others, if it is exercised for selfish gain or muddy ulterior purposes. We should be curious, though. We should be interested in the people around us. We should like to find out. We should occasionally pry into dark corners. Technical, scientific, scholarly, and often enough social progress has been activated by curiosity. As a general rule, however, be curious, try to find out, but be careful in telling what you found out!

Assertiveness

Do not try to be an assertive lion if you are a timid mouse. Assertiveness must come naturally and is not always advisable. A timid person may be a coward, but an assertive person is certainly a bully. As much can be gained by courtesy and diplomacy, by patience and persuasion as by assertion, threats, commands, and rudeness, though there is no denying—alas—that on rare occasions one must assert oneself in crude and brutal ways. There is a psychological law which works as relentlessly as any law in physics, namely that pressure produces counter-pressure. Love, unfortunately, does not always produce love in return. Self-assertion should be used like the army of a nation: to be there if needed, to be ready, to be strong and powerful, but to be used only in self-defense or on the most heinous provocation and in full awareness of all the dangers involved.

Quickness

Does not lie in the rapidity with which an action is completed, but in its immediacy. One can be slow—and actually one ought to be slow and careful in thought—but one must be quick in action. One ought to delay for deliberation, but once a decision is made one must act at once. Successful people are seldom people who dilly-dally, who postpone action, or who cannot make up their minds. Get into the habit of answering letters immediately, of paying bills promptly, of repairing what needs to be repaired at once. One usually saves time, money, and energy by responding quickly to all demands which daily living makes upon us. Napoleon's favorite word seems to have been: "*Vite! Vite!*" Let your favorite maxim be: "Now!"

Vivacity

Is sometimes hard on those who are exposed to it. In fact, constant exposure to vivacious persons makes one long for dullness, quiet, passivity, and restraint. Vivacity is the prerogative of youth; it must be curbed by the elderly. Nothing is worse than the affected vivacity of old ladies whose vivacity was charming when they were young. The unnaturally vivacious old gent is simply a clown. Yet where vivacity is genuine, where it is not self-conscious, where the vivacious person is really unaware of his or her vivacity, there it will be charming. So, if you think you are vivacious by nature, be animated but not explosive; enthusiastic but not ecstatic; joyful but not crazy and, when circumstances demand it, sad but not hysterical.

Spontaneity

Is a double-edged sword. Spontaneous actions have caused as much harm as help. Too much hesitancy and procrastination is as bad as heedless action. The general rule is that spontaneity is always justified and good where it springs from noble impulses and high endeavor. Indeed, such spontaneity is laudable; whether it is felicitous and advantageous is another question. Unfortunately, we no longer live in times where a good conscience is its own reward. Also, the world is full of crooks who are waiting to profit from our spontaneity. Therefore, be as spontaneous as compatible with goodness, taste, and tact within the circle of your family, your relatives and friends, but be circumspect and wary with strangers. And, always resist where you feel that your spontaneity is appealed to for political, religious, or commercial ends.

Wealth

Is neither a virtue nor a disgrace. It all depends upon the ways in which it was acquired and upon the manner in which it is spent. In fact, it may be argued that it is easier to be charitable, generous, and good with money than without it. What distinguishes the wealthy from the poor is power, hence the assurance and self-confidence of the rich. Yet a new age is dawning in which wealth may be a liability. The wealthy are besieged today and increasingly forced to lead simple lives, to avoid ostentation, to be invisible and anonymous. Their wealth is resented and bandits, terrorists, and revolutionaries are out to get them. Still, government by the rich of old wealth is preferable to that of the ambitious poor who, for good and understandable reasons, are often petty, vindictive, and doctrinaire once they are in power.

Help

Freely given and—one hopes—gratefully acknowledged is a form of love and therefore one of the strongest social bonds, perhaps the strongest. Lonely giants do not survive, but pygmies do who help each other. There are, however, some reservations: help given unwittingly does not make happy; help given with an expectation of thanks will bring disappointment; in fact, help may beget hostility. Hitler as a poor young man was helped by some kindly Jews and hated all Jews ever after. In helping another person, try to make him or her self-supporting and independent. Offer help once or twice and no more. Do not expect gratitude. If you receive help, acknowledge it joyfully and immediately. And, do not forget the old saying that help given promptly is help given twice.

Influence

As in Dale Carnegie's famous *How to Win Friends and Influence People* is a polite word for manipulation. Manipulation sounds awful and that is why we did not name this entry "Manipulation." Manipulating others is, of course, what we do all the time, must do all the time either by threats, promises, commands, suggestions, rewards, judgments, and sermons, or by observing law and custom and thus avoiding clashes with police and neighbors. We interact with others all the time—even hermits do—and we cannot but react to their words and deeds and thoughts in such a way that these will redound to our pleasure and advantage. Manipulation is only the conscious and extremely selfish actualization of a natural process which goes on continually and without which we could not survive.

Reciprocity—

The life of natural man is based upon reciprocity. You do me a favor, I shall do you a favor. You are nasty to me, I shall be nasty to you. Love, of course, supersedes reciprocity. (You are nasty to me and I still love you.) It is good to remember that reciprocity is the natural order of things. One often finds nice and intelligent people, especially younger ones, who unaccountably find themselves lonely and abandoned. Why? No reciprocity: they were invited, but it never struck them that they have to invite in return. They did not answer letters. They took favors for granted. As long as man is imperfect, reciprocity is enormously important. The essence of being spoilt is never to show any reciprocity.

Conviviality

Is based on a few simple rules: one must always answer an invitation accepting or declining it. No reasons need be given for declining. In accepting an invitation one enters an unwritten social contract which obliges one either to bring a gift (flowers, a bottle of wine, a box of candy) or to write a note of thanks or to invite in return. When you have guests, never try to impose your idea of a good time upon them. The main point of any party is talk, the creation of a feeling of well-being and good fellowship. All of us need the stimulus of a good party from time to time in the same way we need a vacation or the stimulus of art. Give all your guests a chance to shine. Be natural as host or guest and do not look upon a party as a war game, a man (or woman) hunt, a business proposition, or an occasion for drunken excess.

Renunciation—

A difficult art, but one which we have to perfect in the course of our lives. Quite naturally, we must renounce so many things as we grow older: parents must renounce their children once the children have grown up, men must renounce their jobs once they have reached retirement age, most women will be widows one day, and both sexes will have to renounce the many pleasures which the body and its senses offered. When the break comes, make it forthrightly; do not go back to visit the old firm, do not see your children unless they want you to come, do not entertain foolish romances when your time is past. However, compensate! If you can't play tennis anymore, walk. If you can't take care of your family anymore, take care of others. If your own renunciation is too bitter, visit those who are worse off: the blind, the crippled, the terminally ill.

Regret

As remorse is, of course, good and necessary. Where we have done something wrong or where we have caused some hurt or harm, we ought not only to apologize but offer to make restitution. Simply to say: "Sorry!" may not be enough. There is, however, another kind of regret which must be avoided under all circumstances and that is regret as self-pity. It is the "if only" kind of regret: if only I had bought Xerox stock twenty years ago, if only I had chosen another man (or wife) or another career, if only I had not done such and such foolish or fatal thing. This kind of regret is soul-destroying. One must force oneself to forget those mishaps and misfortunes and, with some effort of will, one can do so. Nature helps us. Sleep heals. Time is on our side.

Idealism

Is a worldly religion. It provides a vision of a higher life, of a more perfect society, of justice, peace, and happiness. Idealism is always based on a belief in the perfectibility of man, though history and anthropology offer no guidelines to judge the efficacy of idealism. A case may be made for the assertion that mankind today is indeed a bit better and more civilized than in the past. (No more officially endorsed slavery, for instance.) On the other hand, a case may also be made for the intractable wickedness of man. In default of traditional religious belief (which anyhow did not prevent the most atrocious barbarities), we have to abide by a humane and skeptical idealism which still sustains man's brightest hopes.

Inspiration—

"Breathing into"—the divine afflatus—the very word means breath and air and rushing movement. Inspiration in modern times is seen as part of our supersensible ability, of our supranormal faculties. Every thought is an inspiration, from the most trivial to the most sublime. There is little we can do to help us get inspiration, though every creative person develops little tricks and stratagems to keep the mind open for heavenly hints. Concentration helps some people and hinders others; noise, motion, change, and entertainment aid some, while others must have calm, quiet, and seclusion. It is sometimes helpful when trying to get to A to pursue B, as one sees certain stars at the margin of the telescope field not by looking directly at them, but by looking at another star nearby.

Piety

Was once the virtue of virtues. As long as the great symbolical systems of the major religions were tacitly accepted, were indeed the only forms under which Man and World were understood, an adherence to the moral precepts of such a religion was necessary, good, and right. Heretics, under these circumstances, were viewed with the same horror with which we consider terrorists or criminals. The overreaching systems have disappeared. It is difficult to demand obedience to the laws of a divinity which one no longer senses or in which one does not believe. We have to return to the Roman concept of *pietas*, which meant the reverential preservation and cultivation of traditional values, of custom, order, decency, and commonly understood morality, until God or the gods will speak to us again and we shall no longer assume but know.